Cameron Mackintosh Presents
Boublil and Schönberg's

Selections From
Les Misérables

A Musical by
Alain Boublil & Claude-Michel Schönberg

Lyrics by Herbert Kretzmer

based on the novel by VICTOR HUGO

Music by CLAUDE-MICHEL SCHÖNBERG
Lyrics by HERBERT KRETZMER
Original French text by ALAIN BOUBLIL
and JEAN-MARC NATEL
Additional material by JAMES FENTON

Orchestral score by JOHN CAMERON
Production Musical Supervisor ROBERT BILLIG
Musical Director JAMES MAY
Sound by ANDREW BRUCE/AUTOGRAPH

Associate Director and Executive Producer
RICHARD JAY-ALEXANDER
Executive Producer MARTIN McCALLUM
Casting by JOHNSON-LIFF & ZERMAN
General Management ALAN WASSER

Designed by JOHN NAPIER
Lighting by DAVID HERSEY
Costumes by ANDREANE NEOFITOU

Directed and Adapted by
TREVOR NUNN & JOHN CAIRD

THE MUSICAL SENSATION
1987 TONY® AWARD BEST MUSICAL

CONTENTS

T0053069

ISBN 978-0-7935-4901-6

ALAIN BOUBLIL MUSIC LTD.

EXCLUSIVELY DISTRIBUTED BY

HAL•LEONARD®
CORPORATION
7777 W. BLUEMOUND RD. P.O. BOX 13819 MILWAUKEE, WI 53213

Visit Hal Leonard Online at
www.halleonard.com

AT THE END OF THE DAY

Violin

Music by CLAUDE-MICHEL SCHÖNBERG
Lyrics by HERBERT KRETZMER
Original Text by ALAIN BOUBLIL and JEAN-MARC NATEL

BRING HIM HOME

Violin

Music by CLAUDE-MICHEL SCHÖNBERG
Lyrics by HERBERT KRETZMER and ALAIN BOUBLIL

CASTLE ON A CLOUD

Violin

Music by CLAUDE-MICHEL SCHÖNBERG
Lyrics by HERBERT KRETZMER
Original Text by ALAIN BOUBLIL and JEAN-MARC NATEL

DO YOU HEAR THE PEOPLE SING?

Violin

Music by CLAUDE-MICHEL SCHÖNBERG
Lyrics by HERBERT KRETZMER
Original Text by ALAIN BOUBLIL and JEAN-MARC NATEL

DRINK WITH ME
(To Days Gone By)

Violin

Music by CLAUDE-MICHEL SCHÖNBERG
Lyrics by HERBERT KRETZMER and ALAIN BOUBLIL

EMPTY CHAIRS AT EMPTY TABLES

Violin

Music by CLAUDE-MICHEL SCHÖNBERG
Lyrics by HERBERT KRETZMER and ALAIN BOUBLIL

A HEART FULL OF LOVE

Violin

Music by CLAUDE-MICHEL SCHÖNBERG
Lyrics by HERBERT KRETZMER
Original Text by ALAIN BOUBLIL and JEAN-MARC NATEL

Allegretto

mf

2

4

poco rall.   *meno mosso*

rall.

I DREAMED A DREAM

Violin

Music by CLAUDE-MICHEL SCHÖNBERG
Lyrics by HERBERT KRETZMER
Original Text by ALAIN BOUBLIL and JEAN-MARC NATEL

IN MY LIFE

Violin

Music by CLAUDE-MICHEL SCHÖNBERG
Lyrics by HERBERT KRETZMER
Original Text by ALAIN BOUBLIL and JEAN-MARC NATEL

rall.　　　　　　　　　　a tempo

2

f *piu mosso*

mf

rall.

A LITTLE FALL OF RAIN

Violin

Music by CLAUDE-MICHEL SCHÖNBERG
Lyrics by HERBERT KRETZMER
Original Text by ALAIN BOUBLIL and JEAN-MARC NATEL

ON MY OWN

Violin

Music by CLAUDE-MICHEL SCHÖNBERG
Lyrics by ALAIN BOUBLIL, HERBERT KRETZMER, JOHN CAIRD,
TREVOR NUNN and JEAN-MARC NATEL

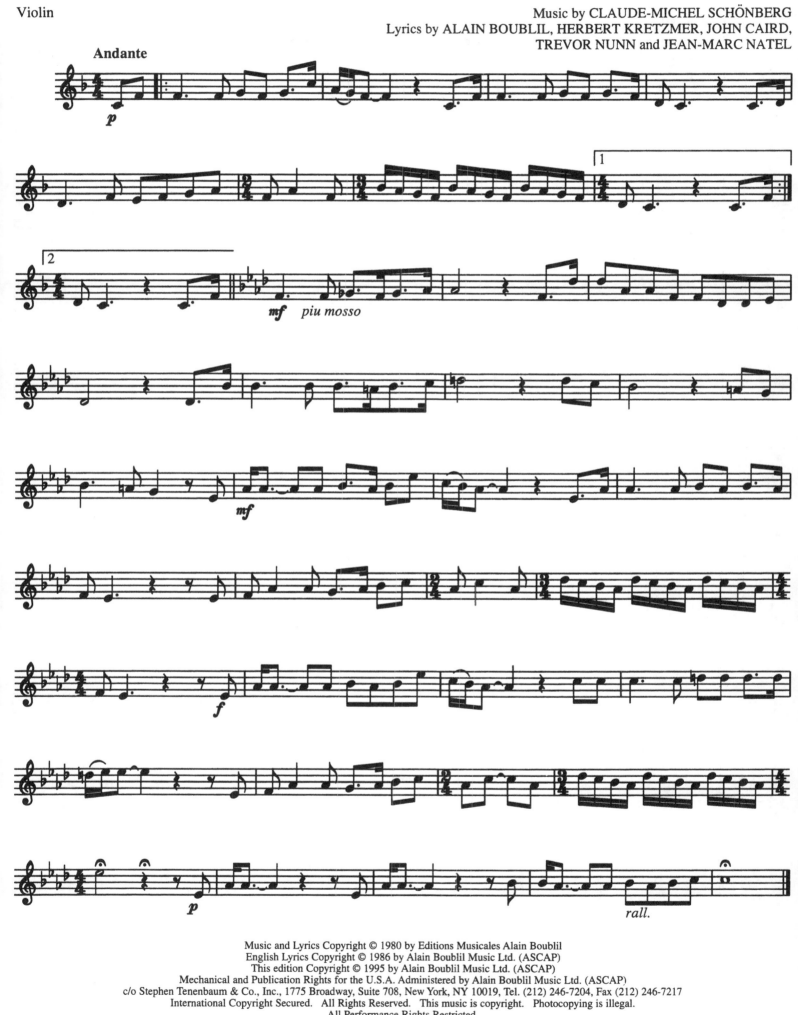

STARS

Violin

Music by CLAUDE-MICHEL SCHÖNBERG
Lyrics by HERBERT KRETZMER and ALAIN BOUBLIL

WHO AM I?

Violin

Music by CLAUDE-MICHEL SCHÖNBERG
Lyrics by HERBERT KRETZMER
Original Text by ALAIN BOUBLIL and JEAN-MARC NATEL